Channel Islands National Park

SUSAN LAMB

PRINCIPAL PHOTOGRAPHY BY
GEORGE H. H. HUEY

WESTERN NATIONAL PARKS ASSOCIATION
TUCSON, ARIZONA

Introduction

Something in our salty blood draws us to the sea; something in our imagination beckons us to islands. Channel Islands National Park encompasses both: almost two hundred square miles of ocean and five remarkable islands. Each of the islands is a fascinating world unto itself, fragrant with flowers and sagebrush and musical with birdsong, wind, and the murmuring sea. They are miniature versions of the California that many visitors may have thought was lost long ago, surrounded by some of the most pristine and wildlife-rich waters in the eastern Pacific. In 1980, Congress established this national park to include not only the islands but the full nautical mile of ocean surrounding each of them *in order to protect the nationally significant natural, scenic, wildlife, marine, ecological, archaeological, cultural, and scientific values of the Channel Islands.* Along with the rich diversity of plants and animals protected within its boundaries, the park conserves archeological sites from almost thirteen thousand years of human presence on the islands. Visitors also rediscover less tangible qualities here: natural quiet, the darkness of the night sky, and a peacefulness rarely found on the nearby coast. Even the air of the islands is refreshingly clean; lichens that shrivel in the polluted air of the mainland grow in lush profusion here.

The closest island—which is really three small islets—can often be seen from Ventura as a dark ridge rearing out of the sea only fourteen miles to the south. A classic seabird rookery, this island is called Anacapa, from the Chumash word *Anyapakh,* meaning "mirage." Anacapa points westward to the massive bulk of Santa Cruz Island, ninety-six square miles of mountain, valley, and beach that make up half the land area of the park. Farther west, Santa Rosa Island and the remote pinniped sanctuary of San Miguel extend toward the open sea. Santa Barbara Island, their tiny but beautiful cousin, lies fifty-four miles from Ventura, to the south of Anacapa, together with three other Channel Islands that are not included within the park.

SEASONS People often say that southern California has no change of seasons, but year-round visits to the Channel Islands prove just the opposite. Away from the insulating factors of climate-controlled buildings and irrigated gardens, the seasons of southern California are much more obvious. They conform to the Mediterranean climate pattern of dry summers and wet winters, with temperatures ranging from the nineties in July to the low thirties in midwinter.

Winter is the green and growing season on the Channel Islands, because it is when the jet stream shifts south to blow rainstorms from the Pacific over southern California. The date of winter's arrival varies, but native Chumash people chose to call November "the month when rain keeps us indoors." More rain falls in the north and west than in the south, and for a longer period of time (winter is much wetter and several weeks longer on San Miguel

Sunrise at Arch Point, Santa Barbara Island, with Shag Rock at right. Goldfields, Lasthenia californica, carpet the meager and exposed soil where grasses are sparse.

than on Santa Barbara Island). The rains quickly bring plants out of their drought-induced dormancy to cloak the islands in long green grasses dotted with wildflowers and stands of brilliant yellow coreopsis busily pollinated by butterflies and other insects.

Beginning in December, as many as twenty thousand gray whales migrate through the area en route to Baja California; northern birds such as Arctic loons and phalaropes spend winter around the islands as well. Thousands of *pinnipeds*—seals and sea lions—congregate on remote island beaches, especially on San Miguel.

Late winter and early spring is the breeding season for island seabirds. Some seabird species return at this time from months at sea, while others remain on the islands throughout the year. During these relatively cool, wet months, the birds develop breeding plumage, court, and bond. They begin to clear out old nests or build new ones. For many species of seabirds, the Channel Islands offer the only remaining nesting sites in California or, in some cases, the world. Because the birds and their nestlings are especially vulnerable to disturbance by human visitors during this season, parts of the islands may be closed temporarily to ensure their survival.

As the days lengthen in February and March, strong winds push the warm surface waters of the sea, and cold, nutrient-rich water from great depths replaces them in a process known as upwelling. Rainstorms on land also send "plumes" of other nutrients into the sea via rivers, including more nitrates and phosphates, potassium, silicon, and iron. These nutrients—together with increasing hours of spring daylight—stimulate the growth of algae and phytoplankton (microscopic floating plants), which form the basis of the ocean food chain. Most creatures in the ocean begin as microscopic zooplankton, tiny floating animals such as the larvae of crustaceans. A chain reaction begins as these zooplankton feed on algae and phytoplankton and are in turn consumed by fish, jellyfish, shellfish, whales, and seabirds, creating a surge of life in the ocean.

Around May, the Pacific high pressure zone begins to block storms from the north and west. Plants fade toward dormancy and the sea grows calm. As sun-heated air rises from the interior valleys of California, it creates a vacuum that pulls ocean air inland. Flowing over the still-cold offshore waters, this moist air condenses into fogs nicknamed the "June gloom." Such early summer fogs cool the air and filter the sunshine, easing the transition on land from gentle winter rains to the scorched dryness of summer. The sea is usually "friendly," or calm, making June a good month to view seabirds from deck during Channel crossings and to perhaps catch a glimpse of a blue whale. Blue whales are the largest animals ever to exist on earth and an increasing number of them have spent summers in the Channel in recent years.

The Channel Islands—especially Santa Rosa and San Miguel—experience a longer foggy season than the mainland and their temperatures are moderated by the surrounding sea. Around the beginning of July, however, shifting currents and intense sun mean a warmer ocean and less fog. Plants endure the full brunt of long days with bright sun and little moisture. By midsummer, the islands are mostly dry and tawny like the rest of the southern California coast, with the majority of native plants lying dormant until the rains return. Summer afternoons bring increasing winds but evenings are calmer, quiet, and cool. Despite occasional plankton blooms, the water is usually placid and clear. Bright orange semitropical fish called Garibaldis extend their range north- and westward, and pelagic fish from the open ocean surround the islands. Many locals regard September and October as the best months for swimming, snorkeling, and scuba diving around the islands because the water is at its warmest, clearest, and least turbulent then.

Throughout the seasons, scientists from a wide array of disciplines conduct research on the Channel Islands. Some investigate and monitor the dynamics of living things both on the islands and in the sea around them. Others study the climate, geology, paleontology, and human story here. Park interpreters incorporate their findings into programs offered year-round to visitors, making Channel Islands National Park a unique opportunity for both scientists and the public to gain a greater understanding and appreciation of the vital processes of the natural world.

California sea lions—the region's most common marine mammal—bask atop molting northern elephant seals, San Miguel Island. After losing up to half their weight during the winter breeding season, northern elephant seals leave their rookeries to feed at sea for a few months. Females may dive as deep as fifteen hundred feet for twenty-two minutes, males as long as eighty minutes. Instruments recorded one male reaching almost a mile in depth.

Throughout the year, the Channel Islands provide critical nesting and roosting habitat for brown pelicans, endangered seabirds that are highly sensitive to disturbance by hikers and kayakers.

Each fall, gray whales migrate about five thousand miles from Arctic waters to the warm seas of coastal Baja California, where the females give birth. Seen around the Channel Islands between early December and January and again during their return journey from February through April, gray whales—especially mothers with calves— sometimes pause to feed in kelp beds. Photograph by Jeff Foott

Life on Land

ISOLATION, EXPOSURE, AND ADAPTATION

Surrounded by waters abundantly rich in marine life, the half of Channel Islands National Park that is on land above the high tide line supports a narrow and fragile range of life forms. Ever since the islands emerged from the sea, the spores of mosses and seeds of flowering plants, as well as insects, snakes and other reptiles, birds, and mammals—especially mice and bats—have been carried out to them from the mainland by water, wind, flotsam, seabirds, and people. Yet the more than seven hundred terrestrial plants and animals found on the islands are still far fewer than the number on the mainland. Because the sea is such a formidable obstacle, the farther an island lies from the source of its immigrants, the fewer number of species become established there. Only half as many mainland plants occur on Santa Barbara Island, for instance, as on Anacapa. The size of an island is also an important factor in determining how many different plants and animals it can support. Larger islands sustain greater diversity. Santa Rosa is remote, yet its eighty-two square miles are also large enough to support six species of plants that grow nowhere else.

The Channel Islands sustain habitats that are rarely intact on the mainland, such as grassy marine terraces, estuaries, and marshes, although close inspection reveals a number of differences between the plants and animals that make up the natural communities on the islands and those of the mainland. Giant coreopsis may be found in only a few small, scattered mainland locations because of coastal development, but it still blooms abundantly on the islands.

Botanists have described at least sixteen communities of plants and animals on the Channel Islands. The islands sustain plant communities defined as southern beach and dune as well as valley and foothill grassland. There are several forms of scrub—coastal sage scrub, coastal dune scrub, coyote-brush scrub, and mule-fat scrub on floodplains. There is variety in woodlands also, with Island woodland, southern coastal oak woodland, Bishop pine forest, and the shrubby oak woodland known as Island chaparral. The availability of water is a major influence on plant communities, especially the intertidal and subtidal marine, coastal marsh and estuary, freshwater seeps and springs, riparian (streamside) herbaceous (soft), and southern riparian woodland communities. As on the California mainland, there are vernal ponds on the islands where water collects in shallow depressions and then gradually evaporates, prompting concentric rings of vegetation into bloom.

As the name suggests, island grasslands are made up mostly of grasses with a sprinkling of wildflowers, sedges, and ferns, made musical by sparrows and meadowlarks perched atop rock knobs, low shrubs, and tall grasses. Mice, lizards, and nonpoisonous snakes rustle through sunny meadows while high overhead soar the hawks, falcons, and owls that prey on them. At one time, this island community was dominated by perennial bunchgrasses with root systems that resprouted year after year. Occasional fires probably kept island grasslands healthy by reducing accumulated thatch to nutrient-rich ash. In the nineteenth century, ranchers introduced

Summer fog cools the Island chaparral and oak woodland in and around Cañada Largo, Santa Cruz Island.

Signal Peak Trail, North Peak in distance, Santa Barbara Island. Island grasses become dormant during the warm and dry summer, turning yellow or brown. Non-native plants and grasses introduced to the Channel Islands altered the vegetation here, but resource management programs carried out by the National Park Service have begun to restore these unique plant communities.

Endemic to the southern Channel Islands, the Island night lizard is listed as a threatened species. It finds shelter under California boxthorn shrubs, which also provide nest sites for several island birds and which once protected remnants of native vegetation from the depredations of domestic sheep brought to Santa Barbara Island in the early 1900s.

sheep and cattle, as well as annual European grasses that compete with the native grasses for sunlight and moisture. Livestock depleted the native grasses, especially in winter, reducing the fuel available for beneficial natural fires as well as the ability of native plants to compete with the annual grasses.

Scrub communities support a mix of grasses and wildflowers too, but they are dominated by many small shrubs, such as coyote brush, black sage, lemonade berry, and sagebrush. While some of these shrubs shed their leaves in summer, others keep their leaves year-round to save the energy and water required to grow new ones. To reduce evaporation, the leaves of coastal scrub plants are usually small, leathery or covered with fine hairs or wax, and often fragrant with resins. Some plants store water in their tissues—live-forever stores water in succulent leaves, for example, while manroot develops large tubers to tap sources of moisture. The islands also support coastal dune scrub in sandy areas and coastal

bluff scrub where coreopsis, gumweed, and island cliff aster grow in sparse, unstable soil. Today island endemics of the coastal scrub community must compete with such aliens as crystalline iceplant, a conspicuous invader from southern Africa that concentrates salt in its tissues and makes the soil unfit for other plants.

Chaparral is named for a brushy live oak called *el chaparro* in Spanish. Chaparral also includes other fire-adapted shrub species, such as chamise, toyon, manzanita, and ceanothus, as well as a riot of wildflowers: paintbrush, lupine, shooting stars, bluedicks, mariposa lilies, tidytips, and on Santa Rosa, Chinese houses. Channel Island trees grow primarily in canyons, where it is cooler, damper, and protected from wind, or on northern slopes facing away from the sun. The scrub, chaparral, and woodlands are especially alive with birds. Island jays, Bewick's wrens, and spotted towhees explore thickets for insects, seeds, and berries.

The islands overlap the boundary between two biogeographic

Torrey pine, Pinus torreyana insularis, *is a subspecies found on the northeastern coastal slope of Santa Rosa Island above Becher's Bay and Box Canyon. Torrey pines are found only here on Santa Rosa Island, with a closely related subspecies about ninety miles away on the California mainland near La Jolla. Some of the pines on the island are more than three hundred years old and their numbers apparently are increasing, but because they vary so little in their genetic makeup, their isolated population is vulnerable to introduced pests and disease.*

Mule deer bucks at sunrise on Santa Rosa Island. The Vail & Vickers Company introduced deer and Roosevelt elk to their ranch on Santa Rosa Island for sport hunting. These mule deer are descended from several brought from the Kaibab National Forest north of the Grand Canyon in the late 1920s.

provinces: the northern (Oregonian) and the southern (Californian). They support some plants that are usually found on the mainland only to the north, as well as some typically found to the south. Certain species of lupine, seathrift, and flea-bane that grow on the islands occur on the mainland only as far south as San Luis Obispo County, for example. The islands extend the range of several plants for hundreds of miles.

When climate changes occur over time, some plants and animals retreat to small pockets of favorable conditions. The islands' mild climate and isolation make them a refuge for species with shrinking ranges that prefer moist, cool habitats. According to the fossil record, fernleaf ironwood trees once grew all over western North America. Although fernleaf ironwood has been extinct on the mainland for perhaps six million years, it survives on north-facing slopes and in canyons because the islands have remained moist and cool while the mainland became hotter and dryer.

Each grove may be a single tree surrounded by new shoots from its roots. Another relict species is the Torrey pine, of which one subspecies is found only on Santa Rosa Island.

Isolation—together with the passage of time—has made the islands a hotbed of evolution. Cut off from others of their kind, about seventy-five different plant species and sixty animal species have evolved into *endemics* (forms unique to one or more of the islands). The number of unique life forms is greater when an island is not only remote but large, because there are more ecological niches to fill. *Dwarfism*—a smaller or prostrate form—is seen in island species of chamise and coastal sagebrush. Some animals have also developed smaller forms on the islands. Island foxes—often seen trotting along grassy paths or bolting for shelter under a shrub—are the size of house cats. Examples of *gigantism* (larger size) that occur on the Channel Islands include giant buckwheat and the Santa Cruz Island scrub jay, which is a fourth again as

The islands support some of the same plants and animals as the adjacent mainland, as well as several species found nowhere else.

LEFT: *Seaside daisies,* Erigeron glaucus—*like these blooming on San Miguel Island—grow all along the Pacific coast from Oregon to southern California. Unlike most other Erigeron, this plant's leaves are slightly succulent in order to withstand the drying winds of their exposed habitat.*

ABOVE: *The endemic Santa Rosa Island live-forever,* Dudleya blochmanae insularis, *is another succulent plant well adapted to salty coastal winds. East Point, Santa Rosa Island.*

ABOVE BOTTOM: *Two-day old Xantus murrelets spend their first few days on Santa Barbara Island before taking to the sea.* Photograph by National Park Service.

large and a more brilliant blue than its mainland counterpart.

Hundreds of ancient mammoth bones have been found on the northern islands. Full-sized Columbian mammoths, *Mammuthus columbi,* apparently swam there from the mainland around the end of the Pleistocene when much of the earth's water was trapped in ice. Sea level was hundreds of feet lower, the channel was narrower, and the four northern islands were joined together in one super-island that scientists call *Santarosae.* Mammoths may have been drawn to the island by the scent of ripening vegetation, as elephants are in other parts of the world today. Over many generations, the mammoths decreased in height at the shoulder from fourteen feet to a mere six or seven feet, becoming *Mammuthus exilis,* a pygmy species unique to Santarosae. As the climate warmed and sea level rose, these pygmy mammoths probably evolved in response to a land base that was only a quarter of what it had been before. Not only would they have required less water and food than their giant ancestors, but they were more agile and better able to forage on the hilly remains of their former range. Radiocarbon dates suggest that pygmy mammoths died out around eleven thousand years ago. Although future discoveries may alter this timeline, they were gone about four hundred years before humans came to the islands.

Some island endemics occupy very isolated and specialized niches. Just two thousand individuals of *Dudleya gnoma,* the little "munchkin" live-forever, survive on a few hundred square feet of Santa Rosa's rocky eastern headlands. The soft and chubby island night lizard takes refuge under boxthorn shrubs only on Santa Barbara and other southern islands. Some endemics are now very rare or even extinct because of the grazing of introduced cattle, sheep, pigs, or rabbits; Santa Cruz Island bush mallow presently totals less than twenty plants in three locations. Such tiny populations emphasize the importance of preserving even small populations for the genetic reserves they sustain.

The special circumstances of islands—their isolation and their limited size—have given rise to a branch of science called "island

The endemic Santa Cruz Island scrub jay is a noisy inhabitant of oak and chaparral environments.

Found on Santa Rosa Island in 1994, this fossilized skeleton is the most complete specimen known of a pygmy mammoth. A cast of this remarkable find is on display in the park's Mainland Visitor Center in Ventura. Shown here being prepared for removal from the island by ranger Bill Faulkner, the original skeleton may be seen at the Santa Barbara Museum of Natural History. Photograph by Suzan Smith-Brown

biogeography." A basic observation of this science is that island plants and animals are extremely vulnerable to extinction. Because of their physical boundaries and limited number of species, the Channel Islands are particularly valuable laboratories for the researchers who study the effects on isolated ecosystems of weather, pollution, introduction of non-native plants and animals, and other influences. As natural habitats all over the world shrink and become separated from one another because of development—becoming islands, in effect—this research grows increasingly relevant.

LEFT: *Cliff malacothrix,* Malacothrix saxatillis implicata, *endemic to Channel Islands, above China Harbor, Santa Cruz Island Preserve.*

ABOVE TOP: *Yarrow,* Achillea millefolium, *coastal bush lupine,* Lupinus arboreus, *cobweb thistle,* Cirsium occidentale, *and western wallflower,* Erysimum capitatum, *along the Harris Point Trail, San Miguel Island.*

ABOVE BOTTOM: *Perennial seeps and springs in the bottom of Lobo Canyon on Santa Rosa Island sustain rushes and other water-loving plants in an otherwise near-desert environment.*

OPPOSITE: *Giant coreopsis finds footholds on the eroding sandstone wall of Lobo Canyon.*

GEOLOGY

Paleomagnetic examination of rocks from the northern Channel Islands and the Transverse Range indicates that they rest on a long sliver of the earth's crust that has rotated about eighty-five degrees from its original position aligned with the coast. Certain rocks from San Miguel Island match some from the San Diego area, suggesting that they were once neighbors. What could have twisted this long piece of crust out of position?

Many geologists believe that as the Pacific Plate slid past the North American Plate along a network of faults, it dragged this splinter of crust clockwise. The splinter rotated like a wing nut, stretching, thinning, and cracking the crust around it, releasing floods of lava. Pillow lavas on San Miguel Island date to the Miocene around seventeen to eighteen million years ago, indicating that early eruptions on this end of the splinter took place under the sea. Volcanic rocks grow younger toward its center: the lava flows, breccias, ash, and cinders of Anacapa Island emerged around sixteen million years ago, to be uplifted later by faulting.

Rotation continues today, bringing the islands closer to the mainland at a rate of over six millimeters a year.

The basement rocks of the islands lay under the sea for millions of years, accumulating hundreds of feet of sediments. Between three and five million years ago, rotation of the crustal splinter began encountering resistance. Still the shifting plates exerted pressure, faulting and squeezing the rocks upward until they lay exposed as a line of highlands above sea level. Weathering quickly eroded the softer sediments of these islands—such as shales—to form gentle hills and valleys, while harder granites, basalts, and sandstones endured as ridges and mountains. Rain carved deep canyons into the southern flanks of island uplands, and powerful waves cut cliffs, sea caves, and marine terraces dotted with tidepools into the islands' shorelines. As the sea level rose and fell over time, these wave-cut terraces stood high above the water or were submerged to form platforms around the islands. Active faults beyond the southern edge of the terrace surrounding Santa Cruz Island dropped the ocean floor into a deep basin.

Layers of rock containing petroleum deposits extend from beneath the mainland coast into the sea floor under the channel. Oil rigs access these undersea deposits along the top of a submarine bluff that marks the edge of the Santa Barbara Basin, a basin that in places is over eighteen hundred feet deep.

Life in the Sea

THE SOUTHERN CALIFORNIA BIGHT   The abrupt, right-angle bend of California's coastline at Point Conception encloses twenty-five thousand square miles of ocean and all of the Channel Islands within the Southern California Bight. The Bight is one of the most conspicuous features on the west coast of North America. Although it averages less than sixty fathoms in depth, the sea floor within the Bight is extremely rugged with canyons, plains, deep basins, and sea mounts. West lies the Patton Escarpment, a dramatic submarine drop-off indicating the edge of the North American continent. This great variation in the depth of the sea floor creates myriad habitats, from shallow to deep, sloping to flat, craggy to smooth, and light to dark.

These habitats are made even more diverse by the meeting of cold waters from the north and warmer waters from the south. The California Current is part of a vast circulation pattern sweeping clockwise around the north Pacific Ocean (it is far easier to sail from Mexico to Alaska via Hawaii than to beat north against this current up the California coast). Carrying cold, well-oxygenated water that is low in salinity, the California Current flows down past Point Conception to bathe the western islands of San Miguel and Santa Rosa in the kind of nutrient-rich waters that sustain squid and huge schools of herring, sardines, and anchovies, as well as the larger fishes, such as tuna, and the sea lions that feast on them. There may be as many as 150,000 sea lions in these waters, making them the most numerous of the four species of pinnipeds in the Channel.

As the California Current eddies back up into the Bight, it develops into the *California Countercurrent*. This Countercurrent draws warmer, saltier waters from the south—lively with subtropical creatures such as a parasite-plucking fish called a señorita— to surround Santa Barbara and Anacapa islands. Santa Cruz Island lies in a transition zone where the boundary between the two currents wanders back and forth, bringing together a wealth of life forms, from sponges to crustaceans, fish to marine mammals, usually found along almost a thousand miles of coast to the north and south. The result of all this habitat diversity within the park is a richness in marine life that rivals that of the waters around the Galapagos Islands, the Great Barrier Reef, or the Caribbean. The islands' coastlines and the submerged shelves surrounding them provide habitat for over one thousand different species of marine plants and animals. They are important not only in their own right but also as potential zones of replenishment for the entire Channel and beyond.

THE INTERTIDAL ZONE   Pulled by the gravity of the moon and the sun, the world's oceans slosh back and forth in their basins twice a day. The most extreme tides occur in January, when the earth is closest to the sun. Sea level can vary as much as seven feet between tides around the Channel Islands.

The shoreline between high and low tide is called the intertidal zone. Where it is sandy, crashing surf makes survival almost

Bat star and feather boa kelp. Bat stars eat plants or animals dead or alive, including even the organic film on rocks.

California sea lions fatten on the fish and squid of cold waters. Photograph © Ralph A. Clevenger

Recreational divers conduct an annual "Great American Fish Count" near Anacapa Island and elsewhere in American coastal waters, documenting changes in the number and diversity of marine species. Photograph © Ralph A. Clevenger

Adapted to warm southern waters, brilliant orange Garibaldi are common over rocky bottoms as deep as ninety-five feet from Santa Barbara to southern Baja California. Garibaldi are a protected species and it is illegal to take them for sport or for commercial purposes. Photograph by Charles Wheeler

THE KELP FOREST

Giant kelp, Macrocystis *pyrifera,* forms beds around the islands in cool, relatively protected waters ranging from about twenty to eighty feet deep. It is the largest of the algae and the fastest-growing plant in the world—up to two feet per day to a length of two hundred feet if conditions are right. The kelp

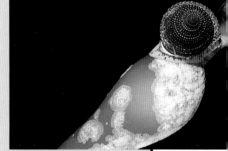

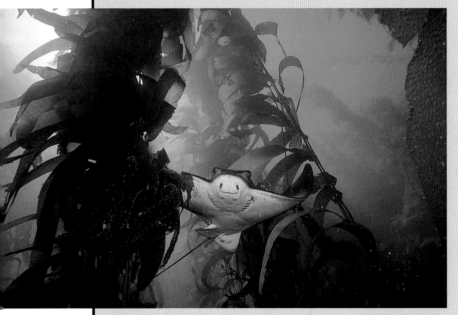

forest is probably the most significant marine habitat in the Southern California Bight. It is an ocean ecosystem comparable in many respects to the tropical rainforests on land. At least eighty species of plants, fish, and invertebrates depend entirely upon kelp for food and shelter; almost one thousand forms of life use it at least part of the time.

The haunting scenery of a kelp grove has been compared to the magnificence of a redwood forest. Even a momentary glimpse of the undersea world is a revelation, its plants and creatures in their many shapes and colors utterly strange and beautiful. Warm rays of sunlight slant down through the kelp's floating canopy, where kelpfish and other small golden fish hang camouflaged among fronds dotted with rasp-tongued turban snails. Schools of silvery topsmelt, halfmoons, and other iridescent fish dart through floating specks of broken-off kelp, molted barnacle husks, and plankton, including the larvae of crustaceans. Opalescent squid circle the edges of the kelp bed, seeking small fish to eat. Attached to the kelp, bryozoans and hydroids—branching colonial animals that resemble colorful, feathery flowers—extend delicate tendrils to comb the water for plankton. Luridly colored orange-and-purple Spanish shawl nudibranchs and other "sea slugs" inch along, preying on the bryozoans and on sponges. Opaleye, kelp bass, and sheephead cruise the region lower down each limpet-scarred stipe (trunk) of kelp; gray bat rays "fly" over the sand below them. On the sea floor, each kelp frond is anchored to rocks by a holdfast, which looks like a lump of amber spaghetti. Over 150 species of animals live in holdfasts at one time or another in their life cycles. Holdfasts serve as nurseries for minute crabs and worms and also shelter shrimp and brittle stars from sculpins, moray eels, and the rockfishes and lingcod with big eyes and flattened chins that are constantly hunting them.

In addition to its role as a lovely and vital ecosystem, the kelp forest is valued as a source of algin, a substance used in dozens of human foods, cosmetics, and medicines. However, kelp is a delicate form of life, vulnerable to damage from storms and changes in water temperature (the 1982-84 El Niño greatly reduced local beds) and threatened by mobs of sea urchins, which were once held in check by sea otters. Since the hunting of otters to extinction locally and the intense harvesting of other predators such as sheephead, sea urchins have created many "barrens" of naked sea floor where kelp groves once flourished.

Bat rays are common fish around the Channel Islands. They can grow up to six feet across and live as long as twenty-four years. On intertidal mudflats, they flap their wings to expose clams, worms, crabs, shrimp, and bottom fish to eat. Bat rays mate in kelp forest clearings in summer. Photograph © Ralph A. Clevenger

Purple-ringed top snails browse on kelp fronds, hydroids, and bryozoans. Surprisingly agile, these snails are able to move thirty feet along stipes of kelp in twenty-four hours and can rear up to attack anemones with their jaws. Photograph by Charles Wheeler

Giant kelp, Macrocystis pyrifera. *Probably only half of the kelp forest that existed at the turn of the century survives today. Forty percent of the remaining kelp beds in southern California lie within Channel Islands National Park.* Photograph by Charles Wheeler

impossible for all but a few creatures, such as sand crabs, clams, sand fleas, and olivella snails, which stay buried most daylight hours but emerge at night to feed. Rocky places provide shelter for a great many more plants and animals: nooks and crannies to hide in and solid surfaces on which to cling. However, the rocky intertidal is also a challenging habitat. Plants and animals in this habitat alternate between being submerged in seawater and lying exposed to the baking rays of the sun or freshwater rainfall.

As a result, the rocky intertidal supports an amazing collection of highly adapted life forms, sorted into life zones according to specific conditions. The main determining factor is how much time a given habitat is exposed to air, although predators from above and especially from below can also limit where a plant or animal will become established. Periwinkles hide among seaweed holdfasts in the highest, or "splash," zone, where surf will not pull them off the rocks to which acorn barnacles and ribbed limpets

cling. The high-tide zone just below that is exposed to air about half the time. Here intertidal algae dry out at low tide but absorb water as the tide rises. Purple shore crabs scuttle past clumps of mussels and gooseneck barnacles, which close up to keep from drying out during low tides and filter the water for nourishment while submerged. Sea stars prey upon the mussels, pulling on their shells in a tug-of-war that sometimes ends as the tide lowers, with the sea star retreating on its hundreds of tube feet into the water. If the mussel becomes exhausted before that, the sea star everts its stomach into the mussel shell and digests it.

Aggregating anemones with their stinging cells form a barrier at the bottom of the mid-tide zone, which is dry about a quarter of the time. Chitons plastered on the rocks scrape off algae for food. Green anemones are very common, their tentacles poisoning tiny animals that float near and stuffing them into their mouths until the tide recedes and the tentacles retract. Surfgrass marks the edge

of the low-tide zone, which is exposed only during those extreme tides of the new and full moons called "spring tides," which are caused when the earth, the sun, and the moon are in a line. Red sea cucumbers may be found here, along with purple sea urchins, feather boa algae, and sunflower sea stars with their many legs.

Tidepools form in pockets among the rocks. The plants and animals that live in tidepools include the same ones that live in the intertidal, plus some that must be submerged virtually all the time, such as surf perch and tidepool sculpins. Blue-footed hermit crabs scamper across the bottoms of pools, retreating into their shells when they sense a shadow.

The areas just below the low-tide line are known as inshore bottoms. Seagrass, sand dollars, scallops, sand dabs, sole, and bat rays are all ideally suited to sandy inshore bottoms. Where they are rocky, inshore bottoms are more hospitable to giant kelp, while rockfish and octopus nudge among the rocks for food.

OPPOSITE LEFT: *Garibaldi, purple sea urchins, and sea star. Garibaldi nibble during the day on reef creatures such as sponges, bryozoans, anemones, worms, nudibranchs, and crabs.* Photograph by Charles Wheeler

OPPOSITE RIGHT: *Intertidal zone, Santa Rosa Island. Ochre sea stars—the most common sea stars on the Pacific coast of North America—struggle to pry apart mussels in a race against time and tide.* Photograph by Dan Richards

TOP: *Brittle stars and nudibranch,* Phidiana hiltoni. *Nudibranchs are molluscs without shells whose garish markings warn predators of their foul taste or toxicity.* Photograph by Charles Wheeler

ABOVE LEFT: *Black abalone aggregate in the intertidal zone. In the 1970s, the California diving fishery turned to these after the pink, red, green, and white abalone populations collapsed, but a withering disease first noted in 1985 wiped out all but a few black abalone.* Photograph by Dan Richards

ABOVE RIGHT: *Purple sea urchins and channeled top snails. The latter usually occupy the uppermost level of the kelp canopy.* Photograph by Jeff Foott

On shallowly submerged rocks where there is plenty of sunlight, plants predominate. Animals—sponges, sea fans, and corals—tend to cover deeper rocks. A sheephead patrols the scene. Photograph by Jim Knowlton

Sea star among club-tipped or strawberry anemones. Although not true anemones, these flower-like animals have stinging cells called nematocysts at the ends of their tentacles. They feed on tiny marine creatures such as copepods and various larvae, and reproduce by splitting apart into clones, forming colonies of identical organisms on the sea floor. Photograph © Norbert Wu/Mo Yung Productions

Garibaldi among hydrocoral. Although they may be seen swimming together in small groups, Garibaldi can be fiercely territorial. They guard large expanses of reef against other fish even larger than their own length at maturity of fourteen inches, rushing at intruders including other Garibaldi and making a menacing sound by gnashing their throat teeth. During the spawning season from March into October, males wait within their territories for females to enter and lay eggs, which the males then fertilize and guard until they hatch in a few weeks. Photograph by Charles Wheeler

Human History

THE CHUMASH People lived on the Channel Islands for thousands of years before the arrival of Europeans. The natural abundance of the surrounding sea together with the plants and animals of the land provided nourishment and met most of their needs, while trade provided the rest. Over the millennia, early peoples left hundreds and hundreds of *middens*—dark composted earth, charcoal, and shell fragments—mostly on the marine terraces of the islands. These middens reveal much of what is known about ten thousand years of cultural adaptation and the ebb and flow of island populations. From time to time, it appears that, because the temperature of the ocean warmed, fewer fish, shellfish, and marine mammals were available for food and materials. When such resources declined, the number of people on the islands may have diminished as well. In any case, the people that we know as

the Chumash grew in number on the islands and their society became fairly complex by around 1150. By 1350, the Chumash had become one of the most numerous of California's native cultures, trading extensively and crossing the Santa Barbara Channel in magnificent *tomols,* or plank canoes.

The name Chumash was assigned to them by ethnographer John Wesley Powell in 1891. It comes from *Tcú-mac,* which is what the Coastal Chumash called the people of Santa Rosa Island; the people of Santa Cruz Island were *Mi-tcú-mac.* Chumash people lived on the northern islands and on the mainland coast from San Luis Obispo to Malibu Canyon, in loosely grouped bands that spoke eight dialects of six languages of the Hokan language family, the oldest in California.

In each Chumash village, a man or woman was invested with the moral authority to serve as wot, or chief. They did not rule absolutely but were advised by *'antap,* a group of people with special knowledge about the natural world and how to tap the sources of power encountered there. The ceremonial clothes of the Chumash were elaborate and imaginative, incorporating elements from earth, sea, and sky. Chumash music, a few scraps of which were recorded in the early twentieth century, is considered to have been especially lovely and sophisticated.

About a quarter of Chumash society belonged to an upper class, among whom tomol builders were highly regarded. They split driftwood logs of redwood or cedar into planks, bound them together with milkweed fiber, and sealed them with pine pitch and with tar from naturally occurring oil seeps before painting them with red ochre and decorating them with intricate inlaid designs of abalone shell and stone. There was also a large middle class and a smaller lower class among the Chumash. These divisions were not only social but economic, with different status accorded to those who performed various roles and tasks.

Shell midden eroding out of a cliff near Carrington Point, Santa Rosa Island.

All of Chumash society, however, kept a close relationship with other living things in the world. Their stories reveal a sense that the sea world is a mirror of the terrestrial world: sardines are like lizards, lobsters are like Jerusalem crickets.

Santa Cruz Island is the legendary place of emergence for Chumash people. They sprouted there from seeds but became so numerous and noisy that *Hutash,* the earth, created a rainbow bridge so that some of them could move to the mainland. While crossing, many of these people tumbled into the sea. Out of compassion for the drowning villagers, Hutash turned them into playful dolphins.

The islanders differed from the people on the mainland in many ways in addition to the language they spoke. They depended more on the resources of the sea than on those of the land, although they probably burned portions of the islands to encourage the growth of certain plants, and carefully tended patches of sedges and rushes for weaving into their beautiful baskets. On Santa Cruz Island and elsewhere, they made drills from local chert with which to manufacture olivella shells into beads, a major form of currency they used in their wide-ranging trade network, which stretched into the Central Valley of California and probably farther. The Spanish introduction of glass beads later devastated this aspect of their economy.

The Chumash people are alive and well today and maintaining many of their traditions in communities along the south-central coast of California. While it is true that the mission era changed their way of life forever, they maintain a vital link with their past through stories. At one time, the stories of indigenous people were thought to be attempts to explain things they did not understand. In recent years, such stories have been revealed as a remarkably effective way for a nonliterate culture to transmit knowledge about a world that they in fact understand very intimately. What seem like charming though pointless tales actually contain a considerable amount of information: which plants to collect for what purpose, what to expect at what season, and how to treat the world and one another. Chumash stories teach their descendants to take only about a tenth of a certain useful plant, selectively pruning it to encourage growth and giving it something in return—perhaps a pinch of tobacco—out of gratitude. In this way, both parties to the exchange benefit not only in a material sense but also in the continuing quality of their relationship with each other.

EUROPEAN EXPLORATION   In 1542, Juan Rodríguez Cabrillo sailed north into the Santa Barbara Channel from Mexico. Some historians trace him to Andalucía, while others insist he was a Portuguese properly named Joaõ Cabrilho, but in any case he was a seasoned conquistador who accepted the offer of Antonio de Mendoza, the viceroy of New Spain, to explore the northwest coast of New Spain and continue to China. The native people his expedition encountered along the coast and on the islands were hospitable for the most part, but his ships struggled against strong winds from the north and the powerful California Current. There were many delays and the local people began to resist the Spanish presence. Cabrillo himself was badly injured in a fall on shore. His expedition resumed the journey north but turned back at Point Conception. They apparently returned to one of the Channel Islands, where Cabrillo died from infection. The fleet again attempted to sail north under a new captain, Bartolomé Ferrer, but above Mendocino they turned back for the last time, having explored twelve hundred miles of the California coast.

Sixty years later Sebastián Vizcaíno explored and mapped the coast of California for Spain. He sought a suitable harbor for the trading ships that sailed from Manila to Mexico using currents in the north Pacific that brought them to the California coast. Landing on one of the southern Channel Islands on the feast of Saint Barbara, December 4, 1602, Vizcaíno named it for the saint.

Coastal California attracted little attention from Europeans until much later. Eventually Spanish authorities decided to establish a presence on the coast, partly in reaction to increased Russian, English, and Dutch interest. In 1769, a large expedition under Gaspar de Portolá moved north through Chumash country by land and sea en route to Monterey Bay, noted by Vizcaíno as a possible port. The Franciscan missionary Father Junipero Serra began establishing missions up the California coast, starting in San Diego the same year. Mission San Buenaventura was founded in 1782. Serra died two years later but his work continued; Father Fermin Lasuén founded Mission Santa Barbara in 1786.

The arrival of Europeans began the devastation of the local people and also the plants and animals of the local landscape. Epidemics of measles and other European diseases wiped out whole villages of Chumash people. Plants introduced from the Mediterranean and elsewhere, such as filaree, began to overwhelm the native flora (researchers have found seeds of introduced plants in the adobe bricks of early missions). Kanakas from Hawaii and Aleut natives brought from Alaska by Russian and English ships established hunting camps on the islands and paddled around in kayaks— called *baidarkas* by the Aleuts—shooting otters and fighting with the Chumash. Hunters expanded their quarry to include whales, fur seals, elephant seals, and sea lions, which they slaughtered for oil, bone, baleen, hides, fur, and even whiskers with which to clean tobacco pipes. During this time, fur seals were locally exterminated and did not return to the Channel Islands until 1958.

FAR LEFT: *Bowl of serpentine stone inlaid with abalone shell.*

Whale and fish effigies of steatite stone, probably used as talismans. Chumash society was highly specialized, with artisans who crafted objects of symbolic as well as practical value.

Chumash and Tongva people have begun to reclaim their seafaring culture, in part through the Chumash Maritime Association's determination to construct three canoes: a traditional Chumash redwood plank tomol, a wood-and-fiberglass training tomol, and a ti'at for the use of Tongva people. As the Association's Roberta Cordero puts it: "Through this we will rediscover the fullness of our dignity and identity as people sprung from this land and nurtured by the sea." Photograph by Althea Edwards and Frank Magallanes

Sunset, west end of Santa Cruz Island, Kinton Point in distance. The Channel Islands mark the end of currents favorable to ships exploring northward. Combined with powerful northerly winds, the California Current frustrates efforts to continue up the coast. The islands and mainland coast in their vicinity appealed early to European settlers; the Southern California Bight is rich in marine mammals and fish, in asphaltum and oil, in grasslands ripe for ranching, and in the fertile soils of a temperate climate ideal for raising grapes, vegetables, and other crops.

Monument above Cuyler Harbor, San Miguel Island, comemorating the arrival in California of an expedition led by Joaõ Rodrigues Cabrilho (Juan Rodriguez Cabrillo). Although the first Europeans to reach what is now called California could not continue far beyond this point, the strong currents coming from the north favored later Spanish ships that crossed the Pacific from Manila to follow the coastline down to Mexico.

Tack room at the Vail & Vickers ranch. The Vail & Vickers Company grazed cattle on Santa Rosa Island from 1902 to 1998.

Archibald Menzies, naturalist on the expedition of Captain George Vancouver, wrote the first English account of the Chumash people in 1793, after much had already changed in their world. Soon afterward Spanish soldiers relocated surviving island Chumash to missions on the mainland, where their way of life was submerged under the introduced religion and routine of mission work they were compelled to follow. By that time, the region had been settled not only by Catholic missionaries, Spanish soldiers, and officials but also by other people descended from many different European nations, who raised crops and livestock, traded, and hunted.

The Mexican government granted Santa Rosa and Santa Cruz islands to settlers during the period of Mexican rule from 1822 to 1848. These grants continued intact when California became part of the United States. Several of those who lived on the Channel Islands kept journals or wrote memoirs; others have been the subject of extensive historical research. You can find books that detail their lives in the mainland visitor center.

Early island owners established ranching operations that remained active for over 150 years. Grantees stocked sheep and cattle on Santa Rosa and Santa Cruz Islands, while lessees on the smaller islands of San Miguel, Anacapa, and Santa Barbara exclusively stocked sheep. The isolation of the islands benefited the ranchers by providing an environment free of predators, poachers, and mainland diseases, but transportation proved difficult. Ranch schooners such as the *Santa Cruz* and *Vaquero* plied the waters of the channel hauling livestock and goods.

On Santa Cruz Island in 1880, French-born forty-niner

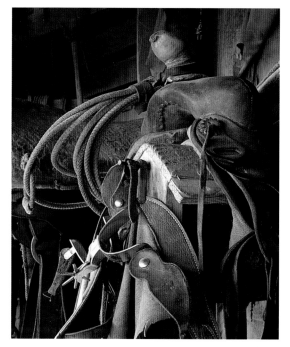

Justinian Caire established a massive and self-sufficient sheep ranch and winery, employing more than a hundred Italian farmers, wine makers, stone masons, blacksmiths, and others, as well as vaqueros from old Santa Barbara. Caire based his operations at a well-laid-out headquarters in the central valley; nine out-ranches, such as Christy and Scorpion, were scattered around the island. Later the Stanton family raised beef cattle on most of the island, while members of the Caire family continued raising sheep on the eastern end. On Santa Rosa Island, the early sheep operation gave way to cattle raising at the turn of the century when the Vail & Vickers Company bought the island. The famous "Island of the Vaqueros" thrived until the livestock was removed in 1998.

Other island activities have included an important fishing and abalone industry, hunting clubs, Hollywood filmmaking, oil exploration, and many forms of recreation. Ira and Margaret Eaton's rustic resort at Santa Cruz's Pelican Bay attracted hundreds of visitors in its heyday of the 1920s and 1930s, and boaters explored the

sea caves and rugged coastlines as they do today. Rumrunners also found the islands' isolation beneficial. The U.S. Army used all the islands for defense purposes during World War II, and the Navy continues to operate on various islands for missile testing and communications. Picturesque Anacapa Lighthouse remains an attraction to island visitors.

As early as 1932, the National Park Service considered the Channel Islands for National Park status. In 1938, President Franklin D. Roosevelt proclaimed Santa Barbara and Anacapa a national monument to preserve mammoth fossils and other notable scientific features. On February 9, 1949, President Harry S. Truman added the submerged lands within one nautical mile of Anacapa and Santa Barbara Islands to the monument. In 1974, the two islands were opened to visits by the public, and in 1976, the National Park Service and the U.S. Navy signed an agreement allowing public visits to San Miguel Island as well. Finally, by an act of Congress in 1980, the four northern islands and Santa

Historic masonry building, Christy Ranch, Santa Cruz Island Preserve. In 1839, Mexico granted Santa Cruz Island to Andres Castillero, who sold it to William Barron. San Francisco investors bought it in 1869; one of them—Justinian Caire—became sole proprietor and established outposts like Christy Ranch where he planted orchards, vineyards, and other crops. In 1937, Caire's heirs sold 90 percent of the island to Edwin Stanton. At first Stanton continued raising sheep, but when he realized how they had devastated the landscape he began to remove them from Santa Cruz. In 1987, The Nature Conservancy inherited Stanton's nine-tenths of the island.

Barbara Island became the country's fortieth national park. In the park's enabling legislation, Congress mandated a natural resources study of the Channel Islands, including an inventory of all terrestrial and marine species, indicating their population dynamics, and probable trends as to future numbers and welfare. Research is as important as any other activity within this national park.

Channel Islands National Park includes not only the islands but extends one nautical mile from each. The marine portion of the national park totals 124,400 acres, which is slightly larger than its land area of 124,115 acres. Channel Islands National Marine Sanctuary, administered by the National Oceanic and Atmospheric Administration of the U.S. Department of Commerce, extends six miles out from the high-tide line of each of the islands, overlapping the boundaries of the national park for one mile from the high-tide line to total 1,658 square miles altogether. The same boundaries contain the Channel Islands Biosphere Reserve, an international designation that provides for the cooperative study of the reserve's resources *to conserve representative samples of the Earth's ecosystems and maintain a genetic stock of the great diversity of plants and animals of our world.*

We tend to assume that everything within a national park is protected by federal laws. However, the state of California has ownership of the seabed and all the marine resources in the water column within three miles of the islands. California has designated Areas of Special Biological Significance around the islands to protect special biological communities by prohibiting discharges of waste to the three-hundred-foot isobath. In addition, the State Lands Commission manages and protects cultural resources, including shipwrecks, from mean high tide to three nautical miles offshore. Marine mammals are protected under the federal Marine Mammal Act, but the state manages all other plants and animals of the ocean half of the park, which includes several commercial and sport fisheries. The National Park Service and the National Marine Sanctuary, in cooperation with the state of California, endeavor to provide the scientific basis and law enforcement assistance to manage these vital resources for the future.

Visiting the Islands

Few people really know Channel Islands National Park, even though it lies just off the coast of densely populated southern California. Maybe the islands' tendency to disappear in the haze makes them seem too distant or dreamlike; perhaps the waters separating the islands from the coast look all too real or forbidding. People may not be aware that there is a great national park nearby, or they may be deterred by the frequent strong winds and heavy seas. In any case, visitors who do make their way to the park often find it to be a delightful break from the congestion and clamor of urban life. The islands are ideal for quiet, uninterrupted time with family and friends—wonderful places to hike, camp, snorkel, or kayak, take photographs, sketch, or just relax to the soothing sounds of the natural world. Campers witness shimmering dawns and often-brilliant sunsets and gaze at stars and planets undimmed by city lights.

Channel Islands is really two national parks of equal size: a land park and a marine park. Each season has its own special qualities and each island offers a very different way to experience them. From December through April, hikers explore islands that are green and flowery and teeming with birds and pinnipeds. Endemic sparrows flit from shrub to shrub while below, black oystercatchers with bright orange bills and pink feet chatter on wave-splashed rocks. Sea lions cruise coves and inlets littered with lolling harbor seals.

The waters around the islands (especially San Miguel and Santa Rosa) are cool in winter and spring, but conditions in the marine half of the park are especially fine during late summer and fall. Generally, the waters surrounding the island are warmest and most clear from July through October, with underwater visibility up to one hundred feet. Seas are calm, although wind can whip up waves in the afternoons and sudden squalls can hit the islands at any time of year. After the fog-prone days of May and June, the islands are bright, sunny, and golden with dormant grasses, pleasant though warm places to picnic, camp, and hike.

PREPARATION A visit to the Channel Islands is an exercise in preparation and self-reliance. There are no services such as food stores or gear rental shops on the islands, no remedies for poor planning once you have arrived. The following checklist may help first-time visitors to organize a trip to the islands:

1. Decide how long your visit will be.

2. Glance over the list below to see which islands offer activities that interest you within that length of time.

3. Read about those islands on pages 34–63 to determine which of them appeals to you most. Check out the park's Internet site at http://www.nps.gov/chis.

Sunset at Little Scorpion Anchorage, Santa Cruz Island, with Anacapa Island and fog bank in the distance.

	ANACAPA	SANTA BARBARA	SANTA CRUZ	SAN MIGUEL	SANTA ROSA
Camping (permit required)	Located up 154 stairs from landing, 7 campsites	Located .5 mile uphill from landing, 8 campsites	.25 mile from landing, 40 campsites at Scorpion Canyon only. No camping on Nature Conservancy	1 mile uphill from landing, 9 campsites	1.5 miles from landing, 15 campsites plus backcountry camping
Day Trips through Concessionairs	Daily, year-round	Spring through fall, 1 weekend per month	Daily year-round to east Santa Cruz, year-round to Nature Conservancy	Year-round extended weekends	Year-round extended weekends
Diving	Excellent	Excellent	Good	Sea and wind conditions often limit to experienced divers. Commercial dive services available.	Sea and wind conditions often limit to experienced divers. Commercial dive services available.
Fishing	Several closures exist	From water only. Several closures exist	From beach or water	From water only. Closures exist	From beaches or water
Hiking	Limited, with only 2 miles of trails open to visitors	Unlimited, with 6 miles of scenic trails	Unlimited, with more than 6000 acres available	Limited, 2.75 miles or longer with ranger	Unlimited, with 54,000 acres available
Historic Sites	Winfield Scott shipwreck, historic lighthouse district	none	Scorpion Valley Ranch and Smugglers Ranch	Cabrillo's monument and Lester Ranch site	Historic Bechers Bay Ranch site
Kayaking	Excellent	Excellent	Excellent	Due to high winds, limited to experienced visitors	Due to high winds, limited to experienced visitors
Swimming (no lifeguard)	Frenchys Cove and the east landing cove	Landing Cove	Scorpion Anchorage, smugglers Cove	Due to high winds, limited to experienced visitors	Due to high winds, limited to experienced visitors
Snorkeling (no lifeguard)	Excellent, good visibility	Excellent, good visibility	Good	Due to high winds, limited to experienced visitors	Due to high winds, limited to experienced visitors
Tidepools	Frenchys cove, West Anacapa	none	Smugglers Cove	Cuylers harbor	Southeast Anchorage
Programs	Interpretive programs available year-round, underwater video program in summer	Interpretive programs avaiable year-round	Interpretive programs available year-round	Interpretive programs available year-round	Interpretive programs available year-round
Wildlife Viewing	Seabirds, seals, and sea lions	Seabirds, seals, and sea lions	Endemic island jay found only on Santa Cruz	Native vegetation and caliche forest	Torrey pines
Picnic Areas	At visitor center and campground	At visitor center and campground	near beach	At campground	At campground
Boating	Landing at Landing Cove and Frenchys Cove	Landing at Landing Cove	Land without permit at any beach on east Santa Cruz, need permit to land on Nature Conservancy	Land only at Cuylers Harbor	Land on any beach except Sandy Point or Skunk Point
Beach Access	Cliff island, no beach access	Cliff island, no beach access	Scorpian Anchorage and Smugglers Cove	Cuylers Harbor	Bechers Bay plus many others

4. Contact the park for information about the island you wish to visit (bulletins include trail map and a list of concessioners). Also request free brochures about your interests: topics include whale watching, camping, boating, kayaking, and scuba diving. If possible, spend an hour or two at the mainland Visitor Center learning about the islands from exhibits, programs, and books.

5. If you wish to visit the west side of Santa Cruz Island, contact The Nature Conservancy (TNC) or the park concession operations to learn about guided programs there. If you plan to anchor a private boat off west Santa Cruz Island and wish to go ashore, contact TNC for a permit.

6. Contact the concessioner to see if transportation is available, and make your reservation.

7. If you plan to stay overnight on any of the islands, request a camping reservation by phoning the National Park Service reservation system at 1-800-365-2267. Camping is free but you'll need a reservation. Book your transportation first.

8. Contact rental shops to reserve any gear required (kayaks, snorkels, wetsuits).

9. Shop and pack for the trip. Clean any seeds or insects from gear and boots to protect fragile island ecosystems from introduced species. Overnight campers should shake out their tents, sleeping bags, and packs to clean them of seeds and soil, paying special attention to clinging burrs and "foxtail" grass seeds. Food and gear should be packed in mouseproof containers even while being prepared on the mainland to avoid enabling animal "hitch hikers" to reach the island. Other suggestions about food and clothing can be found on page 33.

ACTIVITIES

Consider the following activities if you have:

LESS THAN ONE DAY

Channel cruise: Explore the waters around Anacapa for whales and dolphins (no island landing).

East Anacapa Island: Walk alone or with a ranger, have a picnic, go swimming and/or snorkeling.

A FULL DAY

East Anacapa Island: Walk alone or with a ranger, have a picnic, go kayaking, swimming, snorkeling, or scuba diving.

West Anacapa Island: Visit Frenchy's Cove and beach, have a picnic, explore tidepools.

Santa Cruz Island (Scorpion Harbor): Take a ranger-led walk, have a picnic, go hiking, kayaking, swimming, snorkeling, scuba diving, or birdwatching.

Santa Cruz Island (Prisoners' Harbor): The Nature Conservancy (TNC) sponsors several hikes each year, along the shoreline from Prisoners' Harbor to Pelican Bay, along an interior stream in search of the Santa Cruz Island scrub jay, and in the island's central valley. Contact TNC for dates and details.

Santa Barbara Island: Go for a walk, have a picnic, go swimming, snorkeling, scuba diving, or kayaking. Note: Because Santa Barbara Island is so far offshore, most visitors camp overnight rather than make the return journey in a single day.

San Miguel Island: Take a ranger led walk or a walk on the beach.

Santa Rosa Island: Join a ranger-led trip, take a walk on the beach, have a picnic, go hiking, kayaking, swimming, snorkeling, or scuba diving (the water is especially cool in winter). Note: Because Santa Rosa Island is so far offshore, most visitors camp overnight rather than make the long return journey in a single day. It is also possible to fly to Santa Rosa on a day trip; contact the concessioner for dates and details.

Other: Only the park concession operations have the rights as part of their contract to land visitors on the islands, but many dive boat, sport fishing, and kayaking companies offer one-day trips to the waters surrounding the Channel Islands. Check the telephone directory or contact the park for a list of these operators.

If you have your own boat, the area around the Channel Islands is a day trip from coastal marinas

OVERNIGHT

Anacapa Island: Join a ranger-led program, go for a stroll, go kayaking, swimming, snorkeling, scuba diving, or camping.

Santa Cruz Island: Take a ranger-led walk, go hiking, kayaking, swimming, snorkeling, scuba diving, or camping.

TWO NIGHTS AND THREE DAYS

As above under "overnight," with the addition of

San Miguel Island: Join a ranger-led hike, go walking on the beach or kayaking in Cuyler Harbor and camping.

Santa Barbara Island: Go hiking, swimming, snorkeling, scuba diving, kayaking, and camping.

Santa Rosa Island: Join a ranger-led program, walk on the beach (some beaches are closed March 1–September 1), go hiking, kayaking, snorkeling, scuba diving, and camping.

OTHER The concessioners offer summer science camps for children and educational day trips throughout the year; contact them directly for more information. A number of regional museums and organizations, such as the Santa Barbara Museum of

Humpback whale. Photograph by Jeff Foott

Natural History and the Santa Barbara Botanic Garden, offer study trips on topics such as archeology and botany. Dates and details are available through these organizations or by contacting the boat concessioner. The National Park Service arranges field trips for school groups to visit the mainland visitor center or for a ranger to present an in-classroom program at the school. These activities may be arranged by contacting the National Park Service.

FOOD, CLOTHING, AND GEAR Because all the islands involve awkward landings and long treks to campgrounds, pack food and gear in easily carried duffels, backpacks, or coolers with handles. Concessioners limit each bag of gear to forty pounds. For landings on Santa Cruz and San Miguel, bags should be waterproof and visitors should consider reefwalkers or old tennis shoes for the landing. All food containers should be mouse-proof. Plan meals carefully, keep them simple, and repackage your food at home first to reduce space, weight, and litter. Bring extra food in case your return transportation is delayed. There is no water available on any of the islands except Santa Rosa, where some visitors find it has an unpleasant taste. Bring one gallon of water per person per day in containers no larger than 2½ gallons each.

Weather conditions on the islands are very changeable. "Layer" your clothes: plan light clothing for warm afternoons and add layers such as long sleeves, jackets, gloves, and hats for cool mornings and evenings. It is often windy on the islands and during channel crossings. Be prepared for rain between November and May, and bring a sun hat and sunscreen at all times of year. Hikers should have boots with lug soles. Some hikers also wear gaiters to ward off stickers in summer. Rubber boots are handy in wet weather.

THE VOYAGE Every visit to the islands begins with a journey across the water. Part of preparing for a visit means slowing down and scaling one's expectations to island size, and the trip from the mainland is a perfect opportunity to do this. The crossing can be a delightful experience with flying fish skimming over the water and hundreds of common dolphins converging to play in the boat's bow wave. Twenty-six species of whales and porpoises inhabit the Channel, and the chances of seeing some of them are good, either from the deck of a vessel or from the air during concession flights to the islands.

Many visitors sail their own boats, are familiar with the ocean, and enjoy the crossing. On the other hand, visitors who take concession trips to the islands may be anxious about spending hours on a boat. Be as rested as possible if this is an unfamiliar experience, and bring warm clothes, a hat, and a windbreaker because you may need them at any time of year. If prone to sea-sickness, avoid greasy foods before your trip (carbohydrates tend to cause fewer problems) and stay outside in the fresh air during the crossing, keeping your eyes on the horizon. Read the instructions on any preferred remedies before the trip (many pills should be taken well ahead of time). Weather patterns on the ocean can change quickly and dramatically; visitors should be prepared for windy conditions any time of year.

Local concessioners also provide transportation in small planes to Santa Rosa Island. Again, pack light, be rested, and come prepared if you are prone to motion sickness.

RARELY SEEN FROM THE MAINLAND,

Santa Barbara Island

SANTA BARBARA IS

a grassy, gently rolling tableland of about one square mile, surrounded by lichen-encrusted bluffs. The entire island is a marine terrace originally formed by volcanic activity about twenty million years ago, lifted clear of the sea by faulting, and submerged again until the Pleistocene. Its two highest points, 635-foot Signal Peak and 562-foot North Peak, are mere swells along a low ridgeline that bisects the landscape into a rugged east and smoothly sloping west. This ridgeline continues offshore as spiky Shag Rock to the north and picturesque Sutil Rock to the south. You can see and hear the sea from any point on the island, surging and foaming around the ragged lava promontories of Webster Point on the west side and Arch Point on the east.

The California Countercurrent swirls up around Santa Barbara Island all year, bathing the island in relatively warm southern waters. Raked by strong northwesterly winds in winter and spring and often foggy in early summer like the other Channel Islands, Santa Barbara is nonetheless warmer overall, with high temperatures ranging from the fifties in winter to the nineties in summer. California sea lions, harbor seals, and northern elephant seals rest and breed here, and you may see northerly migrating whales around the island as early as February.

Because it lies farthest to the south, Santa Barbara Island is the first island in the park to welcome spring. Most of the year's twelve inches of rain fall between November and April, bringing the giant coreopsis around the Landing Cove back to life and wild cucumber and island morning glory twining along the bluffs. Yellow chicory, bluedicks, and acres of goldfields and creamcups bloom on the thin volcanic soil, which also sustains six endemic species of land snails. Although Santa Barbara Island has no native trees and only half as many plants as Anacapa, it supports eighty-eight native plants plus about forty-five exotics. There are fourteen plants found only on the Channel Islands, including silverlace and silver lotus (both unique to the southern islands), Catalina tarweed, Trask's locoweed, and island sagebrush. Four plants are unique to the island: the Santa Barbara Island live-forever, (a shrubby buckwheat with flat umbels of rust-colored blooms), a chicory, and creamcups (a poppy). Matlike boxthorn shrubs shelter germinating native plants and the island night lizard, which is endemic to three of the southern islands.

In 1901, the U.S. government granted grazing leases on Santa Barbara Island. The native flora is slowly recovering from severe damage by livestock and by rabbits introduced during the 1910s. Alien grasses still dominate, however, making up over half of the

---

Webster Point from Signal Peak Trail, Santa Barbara Island.

Hikers approach Webster Point, surrounded by songbirds, wildflowers, and solitude. Photograph by Tim Hauf

Santa Barbara and Anacapa Islands are the only nesting places for endangered brown pelicans on the Pacific coast of the United States. During nesting season, parts of the islands are off-limits to visitors in order to avoid disturbing these and other nesting birds.

island's vegetation. On the bright side, the numbers of island night lizards, endemic birds, and island deer mice are also recovering since the eradication of feral cats that were brought here as mouse catchers.

Santa Barbara is a bird island. There is good birdwatching along the six miles of hiking trails that wind around and over the island, where endemic subspecies of horned lark, orange-crowned warbler, and house finch may be seen. Harriers, peregrine falcons, and kestrels patrol the grassy mesa seeking mice, crickets, and the endemic grasshopper. Burrowing and short-eared owls also prey in the daytime, and campers often hear the screech of a barn owl at night. Fourteen land birds and eleven species of seabirds—including ashy and black storm petrels, black oystercatchers, and pigeon guillemots—nest on Santa Barbara, which is known for its noisy rookeries of seabirds. Throngs of cormorants nest on bluffs, while as many as two thousand California brown pelicans favor the badlands on the southeast side, where they rebuild huge twig nests in January, lay eggs, and rear their nestlings from February through September. Santa Barbara Island is the only place in all

the California Brown Pelican's range where they literally coexist with people. In June, western gull chicks huddle in shallow nest sites, some of them only a step or two from the trail. The largest known breeding colony of Xantus' murrelets in the world is here. Not much is known about these birds except what has been learned from research on Santa Barbara Island. In spring twilight, Xantus' murrelets mass on the water and sing before returning to their nests in crevices and on shrubs.

For centuries, Santa Barbara Island was a stopover between Santa Catalina and San Nicolas Islands for the Tongva people (formerly called the Gabrieliño) and for the Chumash as well. Although the absence of freshwater and fuelwood kept them from settling here, these pre-Columbian people left evidence of their presence at thirty or so shell middens.

The Landing Cove, the only access to the water, offers good swimming, snorkeling, and tidepooling. Surrounded by relatively shallow shelf basins and patches of kelp forest, offshore Santa Barbara is lively with creatures native to the warmer waters of the California coast: bluebanded goby, yellowfin, and barracuda. The

Santa Barbara Island offers a lesson in optimism. Once feared lost, native plants and animals of the island are recovering since the removal of introduced sheep, rabbits, and cats. Only one square mile in size, Santa Barbara Island supports a swelling population of peregrine falcons, orange-crowned sparrows, native ground-dwelling bees, ladybug beetles, and rare plants such as the Island coastal sagebrush found only on the Channel Islands.

Giant coreopsis in full bloom at sunrise on Santa Barbara Island, Arch Point in the distance. These giant tree sunflowers were beaten back by grazing animals but now blossom abundantly on the island, providing perches for songbirds heard calling all day here.

Santa Barbara Island live-forever, Dudleya traskiae, is an endangered species found only on Santa Barbara Island. Although they produce flowers and seeds, in difficult conditions succulents like these often reproduce by clones at their base.

37

Visitors can completely explore the tiny island of Santa Barbara in just a day or two. Nevertheless, the island can be an entirely different place to different people depending upon their interests. Walkers can explore the scenery from dawn to dusk, birders can watch and listen for seabirds, passerines, and raptors, and flower-lovers may find much to delight their eye in early spring. The warmer waters surrounding the island invite swimmers, snorkelers, kayakers, sailors, and people perched on the cliffs above to enjoy their clarity along with sea lions, diving birds, and Garibaldi.

LEFT: *Sutil Rock from Santa Barbara Island with lichen covered rocks near Signal Peak in the foreground.*

OPPOSITE LEFT: *Goldfields blooming at dawn, Arch Point.*

OPPOSITE RIGHT: *The campground on Santa Barbara Island.* Photograph by Tim Hauf

OPPOSITE RIGHT, BELOW: *Snorkeling off Santa Barbara Island.* Photograph by Tim Hauf

island's volcanic cliffs and dark sand mean good visibility under water. Kayakers can easily circumnavigate Santa Barbara's five-mile coastline, where layers of craggy black basalt have eroded into caves and arches and curious sea lions swim around the boats. (To protect nesting seabirds, do not enter sea caves and stay at least 100 yards away from nesting areas indicated on the map from March until August.) In contrast to the other islands, the best season for kayaking is from about April to June; late-summer kayaking can be rough because of southerly swells.

ACCESS AND FACILITIES: 54 miles from Ventura, about four hours. Concessioner offers day trips and multiple-day trips for campers. Santa Barbara Island is also popular with private

boaters who sail from the Los Angeles area. Visitors climb a ladder to the dock from an untied boat, then hike up a switchback trail that includes 131 steps. The campground is a quarter mile from the top of this trail. There is no water or food available, but ocean breezes cool visitors on warm afternoons. Facilities include a visitor center with exhibits, a campground with picnic tables and pit toilets, and five miles of trails (which are subject to seasonal closures in certain areas to protect nesting birds).

ACTIVITIES: Go birding, hiking, kayaking, snorkeling, scuba diving, camping; take photographs or sketch; search for flowers; watch marine mammals; watch the dawn or sunset; gaze at the stars.

39

CRAGGY ANACAPA IS BUT A TOEHOLD

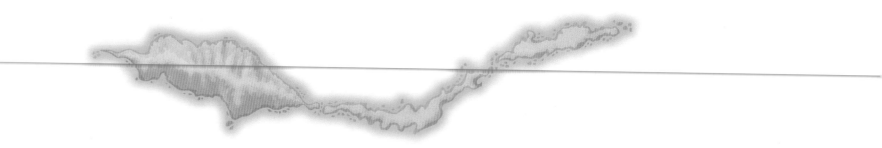

Anacapa Island

IN THE CHANNEL, a five-mile ridge of black cliffs formed of lava that erupted under the sea about sixteen million years ago. Although its total land area is just over one square mile, Anacapa is split into three small islets that are inaccessible from one another. West Anacapa's Summit Peak towers 936 feet, intercepting an average of thirteen inches of rain each year from clouds that drift on to shower only about eight inches on Middle and East Anacapa. The islets support 265 species of plants, including two endemic chicories and a few Catalina cherry, island oak, and toyon trees huddled in the protected canyons of West Anacapa. About 20 percent of Anacapa's plants are non-native species, covering about a fourth of the land area. The native plants suffered when sheep grazed here but have begun to recover on their own with the end of sheep grazing and the Coast Guard era. The park has assisted in slowing the spread of the ice plant introduced by the Coast Guard. Anacapa is home to an endemic deer mouse as well as to twenty plants and eight birds found only on the Channel Islands.

The islets of Anacapa are important bird rookeries, predator-free sanctuaries of steep bluffs streaked with the telltale guano of six species of nesting seabirds. Double-crested, pelagic, and Brandt's cormorants nest on the cliffs from March to August and stand on rock outcrops with their wings spread out to dry in all seasons. West Anacapa is a critical nesting site for California brown pelicans in May and June, when the tilted surface of East Anacapa is also dotted with the nests and fluffy, speckled nestlings of western gulls. Twenty-two species of land birds also nest on Anacapa; many migrants flit about the island as well.

The Chumash people visited Anacapa often enough, as can be seen from twenty-nine middens of abalone and other shells. They did not settle here, however, probably because there is no water or firewood on the island. Gaspar de Portolá noted Anacapa in his log of 1769, calling the three islets Las Mesitas, or "the little tablelands." Various fishermen, marine mammal hunters, and ranchers used the island until 1937. In 1912, the Coast Guard built the present lighthouse as well as quarters that now house year-round park personnel.

The waters around East Anacapa's Landing Cove enjoy a rare distinction: about 125 acres of them are fully protected. No fishing or taking of any creature is permitted in this area. On scheduled summer days, nondivers on Anacapa's dock and in the mainland Visitor Center can experience this undersea world via a live interactive

Sunset's reflected glow on the Anacapa Light, East Anacapa Island.

program presented by a team of underwater diver/naturalists using a video camera. Members of the audience can ask questions of the divers and hear their replies by means of an underwater audio/video system linked by microwave to the mainland Visitor Center.

In winter, visitors come mostly to enjoy the whales, the birds, the flowers of the island's native plant communities, and an escape from the routines of mainland life. Perhaps they are enticed by the yellow glow of the giant coreopsis, which blooms from February into March or April and can sometimes be seen from the mainland. Ice plant has showy flowers also, but this non-native plant will gradually be eradicated. It is often windy on Anacapa in the winter, and the temperature can drop into the thirties at night, but winter offers an opportunity for solitude, quiet walks around the island, and contemplation of the spectacular views from overlook benches.

In summer and fall, the temperature on the island may reach ninety degrees. Most of the island's vegetation is brown and dormant from May through November. The temperature of the surrounding water can be as warm as seventy-two degrees, and underwater visibility is often excellent because the volcanic rock weathers into dark sand that does not reflect light. Summer and fall are good times of year for swimmers to enjoy the Landing Cove and for snorkelers to experience the rich variety of life in the kelp forest. Visibility is best from midsummer into fall because fewer storms churn up the bottom and there are fewer of the algae blooms because of upwelling that are common in early summer. Off the north side of Middle Anacapa, snorkelers and divers can explore the wreck of the *Winfield Scott*, which sank in 1853. Curious sea lions with dark, intelligent eyes and pointed snouts often approach divers and have been known to blow bubbles at their face masks. Anacapa is also a kayaker's paradise where waves have carved an

Ringed by precipitous bluffs, the coastline of Anacapa Island is amazingly rugged with many jagged and half-submerged rocks just offshore. Seals and sea lions find refuge along the craggy shoreline and occasional smooth beaches below the island's sheer cliffs. Ice plant introduced from southern Africa cloaks parts of Anacapa, but an eradication program is underway to restore the native vegetation here.

The most-visited of all the Channel Islands, East Anacapa offers a full schedule of ranger-led programs that interpret the natural and human history of the islands. Even a one-day trip to the island can be a learning experience as well as a pleasure cruise. Photograph by Michael McFadden

A lone sentinel on the eastern crest of the islet, the Anacapa Light, built in 1912, still warns ships away from the treacherous volcanic rocks that surround Anacapa.

intricate array of coves, headlands, blowholes, lava tubes, arches, and 135 sea caves into the island's ten miles of shoreline.

ACCESS AND FACILITIES: Eleven miles from Oxnard, fourteen miles from Ventura, about one to one-and-a-half hours. Most people visit East Anacapa, a narrow, vegetated platform about 150 acres in size. Middle Anacapa is accessible to visitors for escorted use; contact the mainland Visitor Center for details on ranger- and volunteer-led trips to this island. The beach and tidepools around Frenchy's Cove on West Anacapa may be visited only during daylight hours. All the rest of rugged West Anacapa is off-limits to human visitors to protect the largest breeding colony of endangered California brown pelicans. For the same reason, the waters along the north and northeast shores of West Anacapa are closed to boaters out to a depth of 120 feet from January through October.

EXPLORING TIDEPOOLS

- Find out when there will be a low tide. This is the best time to visit.

- Keep an eye on the waves, as the surge can sneak up on you. Wear the proper clothing and expect to get a little wet.

- Watch your step! The rocks can be slippery, and there may be small animals on the rocks that you will harm if you step on them.

- Bring field guides to help you identify the animals.

- Take your time to look carefully. Tidepool organisms are often very small and camouflaged.

- Avoid disturbing the delicate tidepool organisms. It is against the law to collect, harass, feed, or otherwise harm the native wildlife in a national park.

Photograph by Dan Richards

ABOVE: *Aerial view of Arch Rock and East Anacapa Island.*

RIGHT: *The view west from Inspiration Point is especially dramatic at sunrise. Waves continue to shape the volcanic foundations of the three islets of Anacapa. Although together they are larger than Santa Barbara Island, less of Anacapa's total area is accessible to visitors when restrictions for the protection of natural resources are considered.*

OPPOSITE LEFT: *Giant coreopsis outshines the iceplant above Cathedral Cove.*

OPPOSITE RIGHT: *Visitors arriving and departing the dock at Anacapa Island.*

OPPOSITE RIGHT BELOW: *Western gull with its newborn chick, Anacapa Island.*

The park concessioner offers half-day, full-day, and multiple-day return trips for campers to East Anacapa and full-day trips to Frenchy's Cove during optimum tides for tidepooling (prepare for a potentially wet landing by skiff). Visitors to East Anacapa climb a ladder from an untied boat to the dock in the Landing Cove, take 154 steps up to the top of the island, then a half-mile trail to the campground. There are no supplies available on Anacapa, but there is a Visitor Center with exhibits that include the original Fresnel lens from the island's lighthouse, as well as a campground, one and a half miles of nature trail—guided walks offered, trail brochure available—and a historic lighthouse owned and run by the Coast Guard (which is off limits to visitors).

ACTIVITIES: Go birding, strolling, kayaking, snorkeling, scuba diving, camping; take photographs or sketch; search for flowers; watch marine mammals; watch the dawn or sunset; gaze at the stars. Ranger-led walks on weekends (seven days a week during peak season), interactive video program on scheduled summer days.

SANTA CRUZ ISLAND IS A HUNK OF WILD CALIFORNIA BIG ENOUGH TO

Santa Cruz Island

GET LOST IN, encompassing over sixty thousand acres, or almost one hundred square miles. The eastern end of the island is federal land managed by the National Park Service and is readily accessible to visitors. Here more than twenty-three square miles of grassy marine terrace and rugged canyons sprawl below a ridge running from Prisoners Harbor to Valley Anchorage. West of this area, Santa Cruz Island is privately owned and managed by The Nature Conservancy. Visitors who wish to go to this area must contact The Nature Conservancy to obtain a permit to land.

The heart of western Santa Cruz Island is a grassy central valley studded with oak and toyon. Formerly occupied by vineyards, this valley separates two long uplands along the course of a major fault line. Brick-colored metamorphic rocks at least 150 million years in age make up the low, weathered ridge south of the fault. Formed by underwater eruptions less than seventeen million years ago, the dark rocks north of the fault culminate in the highest point in the Channel Islands: 2,470-foot Picacho Diablo. East of Chinese Harbor, volcanic rocks lie buried in as much as fifteen hundred feet of shale deposits that contain a rich layer of chert—a glassy rock much prized by the Chumash for making drill points.

The island's seventy-seven-mile shoreline has many coves and beaches. Volcanic rocks on the northwestern side erode into craggy bluffs with lots of caves. Painted Cave, the longest known sea cave in the world, is named for the colorful minerals, mosses, and lichens of its walls.

Santa Cruz Island receives about twenty inches of rain a year and its coastline is often foggy in May and June. Springs in the uplands, together with rainfall and other processes of erosion, have carved numerous shady canyons brightened by the chirping of Pacific chorus frogs. The woodlands of north-facing slopes are commonly made up of coast live oak, toyon, islay or island cherry, and endemic island oaks, but also include about a thousand stands of ironwood trees. A few cottonwoods and bigleaf maples flourish in northern canyons as well, as do some willows along creek beds. Bishop pines are increasing in number since the removal of cattle and sheep from the island. Non-native Italian stone pines, sycamores, and eucalyptus trees were planted long ago on Santa Cruz Island; some of the oldest and largest eucalyptus in California thrive in the central valley. Finally, woodland fossils on the island, such as cones, seeds, and a Douglas fir log dated at fourteen thousand years, resemble the debris found in modern coastal forests more than four hundred miles to the north. Altogether, Santa Cruz Island today supports more than 650 species of plants and trees,

Sunset along the south coast of Santa Cruz Island.

eight of which are endemic to Santa Cruz and forty-five unique to the Channel Islands. Exotic plants, such as vast stands of fennel, are well established on formerly cultivated land. Nine subspecies of land bird, and the famous giant Santa Cruz Island scrub jay, are endemic here. Among the island's other animals are a salamander, snake, lizard, skunk, and the fossils of a giant mouse from the era of the pygmy mammoths, all endemic to Santa Cruz or the four northern islands. The endemic Island fox is commonly seen here too.

The Chumash and their ancestors lived on Santa Cruz Island for at least eleven thousand years, leaving evidence of their lives in an estimated three thousand archeological sites ranging from temporary camps to ten large villages where they were living when they first met Europeans in 1542. Using chert microdrills—the largest known drillmaking site in North America was at Chinese Harbor—local villagers bored through olivella shells to make most of the shell beads used by the Chumash as currency in their trading relationships throughout southern California.

In 1769, Juan Pérez, captain of Gaspar de Portolá's fleet, claimed the island for Spain. He apparently named it *Santa Cruz,* or "Holy Cross," because Chumash villagers found and returned a staff headed with a cross that had been lost by a priest in the expedition. The following decades of contact with European diseases and conflicts with Aleut hunters decimated the Chumash people. In 1814, Spanish soldiers moved the surviving Chumash to missions on the mainland, and twenty-five years later the Mexican government deeded the island to Andres Castillero. Santa Cruz Island is large enough to support diversified agriculture. Settlers raised sheep, cattle, horses, and pigs here, as well as olives, wine grapes, and vegetables. In 1925, the courts divided Santa Cruz among the several heirs of Justinian Caire, the last private owner of the entire island. Most sold their shares of the island to a family named

Human activity has influenced the vegetation of Santa Cruz Island for at least seven thousand years. Early peoples gathered certain plants for food and materials, sometimes reducing them but also scattering seeds or aerating the soil when digging up tubers. They introduced plants and seeds from the mainland. Settlers of European descent planted crops and raised livestock on Santa Cruz, both of which inadvertently introduced weedy species. Since 1939, however, efforts have been underway to restore the native vegetation of the western portion of the island, now managed by The Nature Conservancy.

FROM FAR LEFT:

Cañada de los Sauces with Santa Cruz Island buckwheat, Eriogonum arborescens, *and Bishop pines,* Pinus muricata.

Northern island bush poppy, Dendromecon rigida harfordii, *Central Valley.*

Checkermallow, Sidalcea malviflora, *among goldfields at Fraser Point.*

Oak trees crowd the sides of Cañada del Puerto.

Willows Anchorage with Ship Rock at sunset.

Stanton in 1937, while others held onto the eastern tenth. The Stantons completed the transfer of western Santa Cruz Island to The Nature Conservancy in 1987; the acquisition of the eastern section by the National Park Service became final in 1997. Historic ranch buildings—some built with bricks manufactured on the island—have been preserved in several places on Santa Cruz. Remnants of livestock present continuing resource problems, however.

Today the majority of visitors arrive at Scorpion Anchorage on the eastern, National Park Service end of Santa Cruz Island. As on other islands within the park, in winter and spring most visitors come for the scenery, the solitude, the flowers and birds, and the hiking. There are several possible hikes depending on the time available (see map). The longest is the trail to Smuggler's Cove, which takes hikers two or three hours on a winding route over a marine terrace to a scene right out of the Mediterranean: an old stone farmhouse below an olive grove, separated by cypress trees and a crescent of white beach from shallow, clear blue water. Ambitious hikers can return via the ridgeline—highest point is the 1,808-foot peak—to the campground, a shady oasis in a grove of massive eucalyptus frequented by flickers and lizards. In summer and fall, Santa Cruz Island is dusty and golden with dried grasses, still ideal for hikers and campers but especially popular with swimmers, snorkelers, and kayakers during this time. Swimming is pleasant after the sunny hike to Smuggler's Cove, and snorkelers may see anything from Garibaldi to octopus among the kelp and rocks of Scorpion Anchorage.

ACCESS AND FACILITIES: Twenty to twenty-five miles from Ventura or Santa Barbara; about one-and-a-half hours. Concessioners offer full-day and multiple-day return trips to east Santa Cruz. Arrival at Scorpion Anchorage requires transferring from the boat to a small dinghy and landing on a pebbly beach or small pier. Half-mile walk to shady campground. No water or

food available. Ranger station and historic ranch buildings; several miles of trails. Visits to west Santa Cruz may be arranged directly with The Nature Conservancy (TNC). TNC offers guided hikes in cooperation with the boat concession operation, including a mile-and- a-half walk from Prisoners Harbor to Pelican Bay, a pretty cove with a shelf of circular tidepools. Visitors must climb a ladder from an untied boat to the dock at Prisoners Harbor or land in a skiff on the beach. Camping is not permitted on this portion of the island.

ACTIVITIES: Go birding (more than 260 species listed here), hiking, kayaking, snorkeling, scuba diving, camping; take photographs or sketch; search for flowers; observe marine mammals; watch the dawn or sunset; gaze at the stars. Ranger-led programs on east Santa Cruz on weekends and in peak season. Special programs on west Santa Cruz by reservation with TNC.

OPPOSITE LEFT: *This old masonry building is now at the center of National Park Service operations at Scorpion Ranch, which is the primary destination of visitors to Santa Cruz Island. Once owned by the Gherini family (who were heirs of Justinian Caire), the eastern tenth of the island is undergoing restoration after decades of use as a sheep ranch and, later, as a private hunting and camping resort.*

OPPOSITE RIGHT: *Built in 1888, this dairy is part of The Nature Conservancy complex at the Main Ranch in the Central Valley. Many of the bricks used in such early structures on Santa Cruz were manufactured on the island.*

LEFT: *Coreopsis cling to the rugged north shore of Santa Cruz Island. Native vegetation—although slowly recovering—is still threatened by pigs and sheep introduced during the last two centuries, which are proving difficult to eliminate completely.*

RIGHT: *A skiff ferries visitors from the boat to the beach at Scorpion Cove, Santa Cruz Island. Visitors should be prepared for a wet landing and have their gear packed in waterproof bags.*

SANTA ROSA IS A LARGE AND WONDERFULLY

Santa Rosa Island

DIVERSE ISLAND.
It has high mountains and rolling marine terraces, miles of sandy beaches, scenic canyons carved into colorful rock formations, fifteen or so perennial creeks, and a unique coastal marsh on its eastern tip. Santa Rosa is remote—beyond the protective lee of Point Conception—which means that its surrounding waters are those of the cold California Current and that thirty-knot winds are not uncommon. Comprising almost eighty-three square miles of uplifted sedimentary rocks, Santa Rosa is separated from Santa Cruz Island by a stretch of choppy water known as the Potato Patch. This increases the remote feel of Santa Rosa, as the skippers of small boats avoid these dangerous currents at certain times of year.

Not far from the boat dock, unpaved roads lead from ranch buildings formerly owned by the Vail & Vickers Company to corrals and stock-watering tanks all over the island. These roads make ideal dayhiking trails. Hikers can take relatively level routes to the beach or to the tidepools of East Point (six miles from the campground), or climb into the island's interior where Black Mountain looms up 1,298 feet and distant Soledad Peak tops 1,574 feet. In addition to the dirt roads, there are several miles of paths, including trails up Water and Cherry Canyons. The lucky visitor may spot endemic Island foxes and spotted skunks. In 1994, paleontologists excavated the most complete skeleton of a dwarf mammoth ever found from a bluff on the west side of Carrington Point. The mainland visitor center displays a replica of that skeleton.

Although 85 percent of the island is covered by a mostly nonnative grassland, botanists are fascinated by Santa Rosa. Among its nearly five hundred plant species is a grove of Torrey pines on the slopes above Bechers Bay. These are remnants of forests that were widespread during the Ice Age. Today just a few pines are left, divided by time and distance into two subspecies: one here and the other almost two hundred miles away in a small preserve near La Jolla, north of San Diego. The cones of Torrey pines are huge, with inch-long seeds that were traded by the Chumash. Endemic island oaks are another relict species that are now considered to be among the rarest oaks in North America. They occur in small groves, either in cooler, north-facing ravines or, oddly, on exposed windy ridges. Although small in size, these groves create tranquil spaces beneath the canopies spread over their massive trunks. Altogether, forty-two of the seventy-five endemic Channel Island plants occur on Santa Rosa, including the two dudleyas that grow at East Point. Carpets of tidytips, goldfields, phacelia, poppies, cream

Looking south from Carrington Point toward Bechers Bay, Santa Rosa Island.

puffs, and lupine bloom on marine terraces in spring. Hillsides are
scented with California sagebrush—"cowboy cologne"—and on
knobs of rock out of reach of grazing animals, there are miniature
gardens of coreopsis, dudleya, and island buckwheat. Dragonflies
skim above endemic red-flowered island monkeyflowers and yel-
low-flowered creek monkeyflowers, fringed Indian pinks, sedges
and horsetails, mosses, and cattails in the shady, moist streambed
of Lobo Canyon. Being drier, Cherry Canyon is home to toyon
and three endemic groups of manzanita.

There are an estimated two to three thousand archeological
sites on Santa Rosa. In Arlington Canyon, archeologists found the
oldest human remains in North America, which are those of a
person who lived thirteen thousand years ago. Santa Rosa was a
permanent home for countless people over the millennia, until the
Chumash villagers of the island were relocated to the mainland in
1817. Santa Rosa was a good home because its surrounding waters
are cold and rich in the nutrients that sustain a rich web of marine
life, from crustaceans such as crabs to mollusks such as abalone,

Only part of the keelson remains to be seen of the four-masted barkentine Jane L. Stanford, *a 215-foot trans-Pacific lumber carrier built in 1892 and scuttled in 1929 at Skunk Point on the east side of Santa Rosa Island. Wrecks litter the waters around the Channel Islands, many of them submerged and seen only by SCUBA divers. The Santa Barbara Channel is still a busy shipping route as well as a year-round challenge for recreational boaters and sailors.*

Bearing sweet, edible red fruits called tunas, a stand of coastal prickly pear cactus, Opuntia littoralis, *is entwined by blossoming wild cucumber,* Marah oreganus, *on the cliffs above Bechers Bay (Santa Cruz Island in the distance). Partly protected from grazing by its sharp spines, prickly pear cactus can take over areas that are heavily used by livestock. Marah—also known as manroot for its enormous, forked taproots—is valued by various coastal tribes for its medicinal properties.*

great schools of pelagic fish, and many marine mammals. Patches of kelp forest further enrich the marine life around the island.

Santa Rosa's coastline has steep cliffs in places, especially on the northeastern shore, but there are also miles of fine beaches. Kayaking around Santa Rosa's sixty-two miles of shoreline is unique in the park, as it is possible during certain times of year to camp overnight on some of these beaches. Visitors are encouraged to bring snorkeling gear or kayaks between late June and October, when they can encounter pinnipeds and other marine animals in the best conditions. Circumnavigating the island is not recommended for novice kayakers, however. Santa Rosa is a blustery, exposed place where winds often kick up dangerous waves. Restrictions on kayaking include staying away from the harbor seals that breed here and can become frantic when disturbed on land. From March 1 to September 1, certain beaches are closed to protect the eggs of plovers, which are laid right out in the open, where they can be trampled.

Streams such as this one in Water Canyon have helped to sustain human occupation on Santa Rosa Island for thousands of years.

Hills rise above the campground on Santa Rosa Island. Photograph by Tim Hauf

ACCESS AND FACILITIES: 40 miles southwest of Ventura. Three to four hours by boat; about thirty minutes by light plane. Visitors may see blue whales or humpbacks on summer crossings, and boat trips to Santa Rosa often include a stop at Painted Cave on the northern coast of Santa Cruz Island. Arrival is at a dock with a ladder that must be climbed from an untied boat. Gear must be carried one-and-a-half level miles from the pier to the campground, where there is running water. Although there are windbreaks in the campground, it can still be windy there at any time of year. Many miles of paths and unpaved roads provide good hiking.

ACTIVITIES: Go birding (more than 195 species listed here), beach walking (some areas closed from March 1 to September 1 to protect nesting birds), hiking, kayaking, snorkeling, scuba diving, campground camping, beach camping by kayak (contact the Visitor Center for more information and permits). Ranger-led programs on scheduled weekends and in summer.

Visitors join a park ranger for an exploration of Lobos Canyon. Named for sea lions—which Spanish-speakers call lobos del mar *or "wolves of the sea"—the canyon is a year-round oasis of hanging gardens, rush-lined streambeds, and shady oaks beneath water-sculpted rock walls. Ranger-led programs interpret the natural and the human histories of the Channel Islands.* Photograph by Tim Hauf

Snowy plovers are listed as a threatened species. They lay camouflaged eggs on beaches, dry mud, or saltflats, where they are easily crushed by hikers. For this reason, the beaches on Santa Rosa where snowy plovers are known to nest, which lie between and include Southeast Anchorage and East Point, are closed every year from March to September. Photograph by Jeff Foott

The northwest shoreline of Santa Rosa Island.

SAN MIGUEL IS THE FARTHEST WEST OF THE

San Miguel Island

CHANNEL ISLANDS.

Lying twenty-six miles due south of Point Conception, San Miguel Island is exposed to the full brunt of the wind and the cold California Current. Fog often shrouds its smooth and rounded profile and the winds here are legendary, endlessly combing the long, thick grasses and shifting the sand around in "marching" dunes. Even 831-foot San Miguel Hill and 817-foot Green Mountain are too streamlined to provide any shelter.

The island is more than just a remote, windswept knoll of fourteen square miles, however. Here visitors may witness wild creatures living as though human beings did not exist. Northern elephant seals, northern fur seals, harbor seals, and California sea lions come to San Miguel not only because its isolation protects them from disturbance but also because its nutrient-rich waters nourish the vast numbers of fish and squid they eat. Elephant seals do not feast during their sojourns on the islands, though. From January through March, these massive blobs of protoplasm rest, mate, and bear young. The males also challenge one another, snorting and rearing and lunging furiously across the sand at rival blobs, stopping to rest every fifty feet or so. But don't let these blobs fool you; they are fast and strong.

Although its twenty-six miles of coastline include several sandy beaches, pinnipeds take precedence along the shores of San Miguel. Humans may land only at Cuyler Harbor, which embraces over a square mile of clear aquamarine water within a graceful arc of white sand beach. The harbor could enclose the whole island of Santa Barbara. It does enclose forty-acre Prince Island, a roosting spot for California brown pelicans as well as a rookery for Cassin's auklets, western gulls, and several species of cormorants.

At Cuyler Harbor's eastern end, low tide exposes a scattering of tidepools. The island is surrounded by cold water that ranges from fifty degrees to the mid-sixties. Jagged offshore rocks have wrecked several ships, giving San Miguel its nickname of "Graveyard of the Pacific." Surrounding the island, divers discover kelp forest, sunken wrecks, and submerged pinnacles. Every rock is crowded with tunicates, bryozoans, and sponges and cruised by a prodigious number of fish.

Grasses—many of them introduced by sheep ranching—are denser and stay green longer than on other islands because San Miguel is so often rainy or cloaked in fog. Flowers blossom everywhere during the rainy season—in spring there are wild cucumbers and paintbrush, bluedicks and blue-eyed grass, island buckwheat and golden yarrow, bush lupine and California poppies, and giant coreopsis in

Basking California sea lions and northern elephant seals near Point Bennett, San Miguel Island.

riotous bloom. The plant communities of San Miguel sustain nearly 270 species of plants. Lush Nidever Canyon is home to buttercups, song sparrows, and water tumbling over travertine falls. Peregrine falcons swoop over trails littered with fox scat, and patches of rushes darken the slopes above the dry lakebed en route to Point Bennett. San Miguel's richness of life seems all the more amazing considering that the island's plant cover was practically demolished during a century of sheep grazing that began in 1850. A drought in the 1870s exacerbated the overgrazing and the introduction of burros after 1942 made things worse, reducing the island to little more than a barren sand dune. Many of the plants to be seen on San Miguel today are non-native, and yet it is heartening to see how the vegetation has recovered here since the end of livestock grazing.

Considering the island's weather and remote location, it may be surprising to learn of its long history of human settlement. The earliest coastal site in North America is a campsite on San Miguel that has been radiocarbon-dated to about 11,600 years before the present time. Chumash people lived here year-round for many centuries, leaving over six hundred archeological sites, from shell middens to campsites to villages. They greeted the first Europeans to sail up the coast of California in 1542: members of the expedition led by Juan Rodrigues Cabrillo. Some historians now believe that Cabrillo died on Santa Catalina Island, but because of earlier interpretations there is a monument to his memory on the island of San Miguel, just off the trail from Cuyler Harbor to the campground. It is inscribed to *Joaõ Cabrilho,* which is the Portuguese spelling of his name.

Visitors can also see a few beams from the adobe of George Nidever poking out of the dirt along the trail to Lester Point. George Nidever was an intrepid mountain man who came to California on an overland expedition and stayed here to hunt

FROM FAR LEFT:

Paintbrush, Castilleja sp., *and giant coreopsis brighten Nidever Canyon above Cuyler Harbor. Cool and often foggy, San Miguel Island sustains a host of wildflowers in spring.*

Several species of cormorants nest on the cliffs and rocky shores of all the Channel Islands. To feed, adult cormorants plunge into the sea and stroke with their wings in pursuit of fish. Photograph by Russ Finley

Hikers can explore miles of trails on San Miguel, although beyond the campground they must be accompanied by a ranger for their own safety, as well as to avoid disturbance of the island's recovering vegetation and wildlife. The only physical evidence of the people who lived here in the past are shell middens and a few fence posts and roof beams, but rangers are well-versed in the human history of the island. Photograph by Tim Hauf

ABOVE: *A member of the iris family, blue-eyed grass,* Sisyrinchium bellum, *blooms along the Harris Point Trail.*

RIGHT: *Owl clover,* Orthocarpus sp.

61

Prehistoric tree castings in the Caliche Forest. Although usually only a foot or two of these "rhizoconcretions" are exposed, some of them are quite large. One log measured nearly four feet in diameter and thirty feet in length. Based on pollen samples, these are castings of ancient pines and cypresses.

Seaside daisies bloom among the dudleya and lichen-covered rocks at Harris Point.

Female northern elephant seals. In 1938, only thirteen elephant seals were found on San Miguel Island. Today they number in the thousands.

and forage throughout the Channel Islands. He became an otter hunter and sheep rancher and built a home on San Miguel. On San Nicolas Island, he discovered a lone Chumash woman who had been left behind when her people were evacuated to the mainland eighteen years earlier. Her story is the basis for the beloved children's book *Island of the Blue Dolphins,* by Scott O'Dell. Between the campground and the ranger station, a few fence posts and depressions remain of the Lester Ranch, once occupied by the colorful Herbert Lester and his family from 1930 until Lester's death in 1942 and by others thereafter. The Navy used San Miguel as a lookout post during the Second World War and as a bombing range during the 1950s and 1960s and will not guarantee that there are no pieces of live ordnance still lying around the island—a strong incentive for visitors to stay on trails!

Although the concessionaires offer occasional one-day trips to San Miguel Island, a typical camp trip to San Miguel lasts three days and two nights. Most visitors spend the first day traveling to the island and hiking their gear up Nidever Canyon to the campground, setting up camp, and exploring the beach and tidepools. The main activity on San Miguel is a guided hike to see the pinnipeds at Point Bennett. This round trip is fourteen miles, takes about eight hours, and is typically made on the second day. Hikers first climb San Miguel Hill and wind through stands of fragrant bush lupine and banks of dune dandelion, reaching the Caliche Forest in just over two miles. Here erosion has exposed an eerie ghost forest of white two-foot-tall casts of tree stumps, formed of a calcium deposit called *caliche.* Some hikers choose to turn back

Windbreaks help keep tents secured at the San Miguel Island campground. Photograph by Tim Hauf

at this point (hiking on the island is surprisingly strenuous because of the strong, persistent wind). Others continue for about five miles to Point Bennett. On the third day, visitors may wish to hike east from the campground to see more pinnipeds at Cardwell Point or north to the scenic grand vistas of the dudleya- and buckwheat-dotted promontories of Lester Point.

FACILITIES AND ACCESS: 70 miles from Ventura, five to six hours. Visitors land in small craft, walk a half mile along the beach, and then hike a half mile up a steep canyon to the campground. Pack gear in backpacks for hauling uphill to the campground and waterproofed for a possible wet landing. Visitors may land without a permit and travel unescorted from the beach at Cuyler Harbor up Nidever Canyon on the trail to the Cabrillo monument, campground, and Lester Ranch site ranger station. Under the agreement between the National Park Service and the U.S. Navy—which still holds title to the island—a ranger must escort all hikers who wish to go beyond the ranger station. Private boaters should radio ahead if they would like to hike beyond the ranger station. There is a campground with windbreaks on the island, as well as the ranger station and twelve miles of hiking trails.

ACTIVITIES: Go birding, beach walking, hiking, kayaking around Cuyler Harbor, snorkeling, scuba diving, camping. Pinnipeds congregate in winter and summer.

As with all the Channel Islands, a visit to San Miguel requires time and effort. Conditions can be windy and harsh at times, although, of course, everything can turn out to be glorious as well. Whether or not the weather cooperates, the reward for venturing out to the islands is a glimpse of a wild and primitive coastal California that is virtually impossible to experience anywhere else. So unfamiliar and yet so close, Channel Islands National Park offers every visitor rare opportunities for wonder, introspection, and adventure.

Arch Rock, east end of Anacapa Island.

Library of Congress Cataloging-in-Publication Data
Lamb, Susan.
    Channel Islands National Park / Susan Lamb ; picture photography by
George H. H. Huey.
                        p. cm.
            ISBN 1–877856–74–6
            1. Channel Islands National Park (Calif.)—Guidebooks. I. Huey,
George H. H. II. Title.
F868.S232L36 1998
917.94'91—dc21   98–27863
                                                        CIP

Copyright © 2000 by Susan Lamb

ISBN 10: 1-877856-74-6
ISBN 13: 978-1-877856-74-7

Published by Western National Parks Association

Net proceeds from WNPA publications support educational and research
programs in the national parks.

Receive a free Western National Parks Association catalog, featuring hundreds
of publications. Email: info@wnpa.org or visit www.wnpa.org

Editorial by Derek Gallagher
Design by Robin Weiss Graphic Design
Photography by George H. H. Huey except as credited
Prepress color preparation by Digital Dimensions
Printing by Imago
Printed in Singapore

Susan Lamb and George H. H. Huey would like to thank the following
people and organizations for their generous help during the preparation
of this book: Mark Connally at Island Packers; Greg Austin, Randy Nelson,
Mark Senning, Carol Spears, Yvonne Menard, Derek Lohuis, Derek Lerma,
Dan Richards, Sarah Cheney, Paige Martin, Don Morris, Ian Williams,
Heidi David, Bill Faulkner, Tom Dore, Jack Gillooly, Tree Gotshall,
Rhonda Brooks, Katherine McEachern, Earl Whetsell, and Diane Napoleone
at Channel Islands National Park; Diane Devine and Rob Klinger of The
Nature Conservancy; Steve Junak and Julie Cordero of the Santa Barbara
Botanical Garden; John Johnson and Linda Agren of the Santa Barbara
Museum of Natural History; Lyndal Laughrin, Brian Guerrero, and Jeff
Howarth of the University of California Natural Reserve System; and
Robert DeLong of the National Marine Mammal Laboratory.